Aspects of a Southern Story

Robert Sargent

Typography by Kathryn E. King
Book design by Ed Lyle

ISBN 0-915380-15-3
LC 82-51069

Cover: Photograph of a wall sculpture created especially
for this book by William Christenberry.

THE WORD WORKS, INC.
PO Box 42164
Washington, DC 20015

ACKNOWLEDGMENTS

The following poems have appeared in the following publications:

"Henry Barry Sargent," *St. Andrews Review*; "Uncle Thompson, About 1900," "Looking for Oldness," "Mississippi Jukejoint: Highway 51," *Cimarron Review*; "A Great—Big—Green—Pickle," *Pembroke Magazine*; "The Wide Bed," *Positively Prince Street*; "The Lost Poems," *Bingo Chow*; "Lending 'The King of the Golden River'," *Southern Humanities Review*; "Today's Poetry: Lesson One," "English 406," "The Epistemologist, Over a Brandy, Opining," "The Brook Cherith," *Sou'wester*; "Circe to Ulysses," *Western Humanities Review*; "Not Yet the Day," *Descant*. "The Epistemologist, Over a Brandy, Opining" has also appeared in *Anthology of Magazine Verse: Yearbook of American Poetry, 1980 Edition*; and "Uncle Thompson, About 1900" (with a title change) in *The Ear's Chamber, An Anthology*.

William Christenberry's sculptures, photographs and paintings have been widely exhibited in galleries and museums both here and abroad, including the National Museum of American Art, the Corcoran Gallery, the New Orleans Museum of Art, the Stedelijk Museum, Amsterdam, and many more. His awards include a fellowship from the National Endowment for the Arts in photography, and a commission from the General Services Administration Art-in-Architecture Program for a wall sculpture in a federal building in Jackson, Mississippi. An exhibition of all aspects of Christenberry's work opened at the Institute for the Arts, Rice University, Houston, in the fall of 1982, and will move to the Corcoran Gallery in the spring of 1983.
He currently teaches at the Corcoran School of Art.

For Mary Jane

CONTENTS

I BEGINNINGS

HENRY BARRY SARGENT
(1844-1914)

Grandfather: a report. For you.
Your current status. 1976.

Your granddaughter lives in Los Angeles,
She's married, has children, grandchildren. In good health.
Little Maud you'd think of her as.
She thinks of you often, with love too,
As an old man in Jacksonville, wife dead,
Daughters dead, one son left in New Orleans.
That you treated her kindly, 50 cents occasionally,
A small child with a dead mother.
And of your little store, Miss Weaver, the bottle,
And Pensacola, the last days.
How you ended up in a rundown boardinghouse,
Found dead on a toilet seat. Maybe cirrhosis.
Maud's who is left
Who's touched your hand, heard your low tones.
Says you had probity. Wonders
About you and Miss Weaver, why you never married.

I think of you too, mostly lately,
Because of this poem, but before this also,
About Ball's Bluff, the War, you and Holmes.
I went there once, not far,
And there, sure enough, was the hill sloping down to the river
You skedaddled down when the Rebel ball
Plunked into your powder pouch. I see you
Seventeen and yelling, just as you told it to Dad.
Holmes was wounded. Gave him a serious view.
I like to read what he said later,

Memorial Day, 1884:
Through our great good fortune,
in our youth our hearts were touched with fire . . .
We have seen with our own eyes,
beyond and above the gold fields,
the snowy heights of honor.
I know you believed this, Grandfather,
Whether you heard it or read it or not.
Grandfather, I believe it, too.

Not much else. And of course Maud and I
Are getting along. However,
In Phoenix, your great-grandson, a rising young businessman,
Bears your full name.

UNCLE THOMPSON, ABOUT 1900

Uncle Thompson Baird, my mother's uncle,
When asked the time by some of his small-fry kindred,
Used to intone:
>   *It is the hour*
>   *When from the bower*
>   *The nightingale's low note is heard.*
I like to think of that.

A GREAT – BIG – GREEN – PICKLE

My florid and affable godfather, Robert Strong
(For whom I am named), delighted in teasing me
When I was a child, say six.
He would turn on me his sternest of looks,
And say, "Robert! I know what you're thinking about.
You're thinking about
A great – big – green – pickle!"
Of course, as this was repeated, I'd whine,
"I'm not! I'm not!" But of course,
After the first time, he was always right.

OUR MOTHER

"It's *raining*, Mother!" Faced with this excuse,
From one of her bookworm children loath to budge,
She'd say, smiling a little tightly, "Well,
I don't think you'll melt."

Or to quiet our apprehension at being lost
In some far place, no one we knew near by,
Would remind us, matter-of-factly, "Don't forget,
You've got a tongue in your head."

We remember her so, dispensing the old admonitions,
Doing her duty, pushing us out of the nest.
None of us knew — we couldn't have known it then —
The need beneath the role.

MY FATHER AND HUEY LONG

My father once took off on Huey Long
At the dinner table, the family sitting around —
I've forgotten what got him started —

I remember it was the '30s and hard times,
Three of us children and Mother, all very quiet,
And Dad at the head of the table,

Commanding the floor as usual, holding forth,
Telling how Huey had told some big shot off,
A railroad czar, I think,

"Rich and paunchy," my father sneered, no doubt
Making it up as he went along. And something
Was scary in how he told it,

His rage. "You g.d. son-of-a-b!" he snarled,
Not cursing in front of the children but letting us know.
He had become Huey,

Venting contempt on some rich proud tycoon,
Making him grovel. My father was trembling now.
And we were all silent, staring,

Frightened, almost, at this depth of feeling, knowing
Vaguely that something hidden was being revealed
Deeper than Huey Long.

THE WORDS OF BAD-EYE PARKER

That's what they said down at the gristmill.
But they kept on a-grindin'
                    Bad-eye Parker, 1932

Bad-eye, it's my understanding you've left us,
According to the college roster.
Some will remember you the bane of authorities,
Blamed when the prize rooster,
Pride of the Agricultural School,
Was stolen and roasted for our delectation.
Blamed when the bells went off all over the campus
(Well-founded, too):
But what I remember these days are those old words
You used to shout into the drugged air,
Waving a bottle. How we laughed!

Laughed without knowing their Heraclitean fullness.
We can speak now, if we wish, from wisdom,
A banked fire,
How we didn't know, when young, of their weight,
Their dark implications.

But really they were better taken the old way:
As defiance howled
Into the Mississippi sky.

MR. BUD IN ACTION

Stymied, the line gang was standing around in the street,
All but the corner pole set. We joked and rested,
Waiting on Mr. Bud,

And all in good time, his time, Mr. Bud drove up
In his yellow truck, heaved himself out, heavily.
A large man in more ways than one.

The foreman said, "Mr. Bud, where you want this pole?"
Pointing to 70 feet of it there in the gutter.
Mr. Bud looked at it, blinked,

Hitched up his pants. We were all quiet now, watching
Him line himself up with the poles we'd already set,
Study the nearby ground

Where the anchors would go, swing himself off to one side
To look down the crossing street. Someone said, "Shhh."
Mr. Bud was thinking things out.

He couldn't have told you what went into his thinking:
Wire tension, guys, wind. An inch made a difference.
No doubt figuring vectors,

Though wouldn't have called it that. Finally decisive,
He lifted his size 12 shoe, planted it down.
"Put her right there," he said.

"Quick! You! James!" the foreman said,
And a small black man holding a piece of chalk
Knelt quickly and marked an X.

Everyone was smiling, Mr. Bud too. The foreman
Could have done it without Mr. Bud. But it was better
To watch Mr. Bud in action.

16

TOUCHING THE PAST

Uptown New Orleans, 1940,
And here was a man of the right color,
Old enough to have been there,

Who maybe heard. So I inquired
From the old man doing his yard work,
"Ever hear Buddy Bolden play?"

"Ah me," he said, stopping his work.
"Yes. But you mean *King*, *King* Bolden.
That's what we called him then."

He leaned on his rake a while, resting.
"Used to play in Algiers, played so loud
We could hear him clear 'cross the river."

He seemed listening. "King Bolden, now,
There was a man could play." We stood there,
Thinking about it, smiling.

II LATELY

THE PENNIES

Afterwards, various things were left
Lying around. For instance, the pennies
She'd collected

In a small wooden box she kept by the door,
Maybe a couple hundred in all.
For a long time

I let them lie there, knowing they were there.
Then I started putting a few in my pocket,
Going out the door,

Shopping, or maybe a trip to the grocery.
The slow months passed. The number got smaller
And smaller. This morning,

I took what was left. Empty now,
Its lid closed, the box sits there,
As if abandoned.

LETTER FOR MY DAUGHTER

Maybe you'd like to try what I just did.
Go to your record shelf, take down the album,
The Witherspoon and Mulligan, has Ben Webster,
The one that we both own.
But first make sure you're alone, very important.
Play it. Sit by yourself and listen.
When it gets to "Trouble in Mind," slow 16 bars,
With Spoon singing, Gerry a solo chorus,
Start crying. If you're alone,
Really alone,
You might be able to do it.

A WOMAN FOR HATS

She was a woman for hats, this brought to mind
Cleaning the closet out. Along with the slacks,
Dresses, coats, blouses, there were the hats,
All shapes and sizes, different colors,
And a floppy white one to go to a party with.
She wore them all with panache, verve, flair —
Look at me in my hat!
Today I am loading my car, finally,
With the closet's contents. It has to be done.
At Goodwill, I'll dump everything, including the hats,
In a large container. Later a Goodwill worker
Will sort out the hats, refurbish where needed,
And put them on sale. And some will be sold.
And a woman somewhere will put on one of the hats
In front of a mirror, maybe the floppy white one.
It will look about as it used to look, floppy.
It will not, however, look as it did when she wore it.

THE WIDE BED

For a long time, I've slept on the right-hand side
Of this wide bed, and on getting sleepy
Have put my book on a shelf to the right,
Stretching to do it. Then I snap off the light.
But not long ago I thought:
Since nobody, now, sleeps in this bed but me,
I can start putting the book to my left on the bed.
And now when I wake in the night,
The book's convenient, easy to reach.
When I snap on the light, the book's right there,
And that takes care of the book.

THE BROOK CHERITH

Today is a day for going
To the brook Cherith,

Where Elijah went,
In his situation,

And was fed by the ravens.
I would welcome that.

But mostly I have in mind
Being alone with the ravens in that far place,

Seated on a grassy bank,
And the brook Cherith

Making its liquid noise,
And the ravens, two of them, perched on rocks,

Quite close, in their comfortable black,
Watching me, I think kindly,

With their cocked heads,
Their blinking, penetrant eyes,

An occasional caw, soft,
As if they knew.

LENDING "THE KING OF THE GOLDEN RIVER"
TO A YOUNG WOMAN

Here is a thin book, old, leather-bound,
Falling apart, almost.
When you read it at your round table,
Snow outside, Anthony messing around,
Think of a small boy in Vicksburg,
Curled up in a window seat, bespectacled,
Reading this very book,
Repeating softly the hero's name,
"Gluck, Gluck, Gluck,"
For the sake of the gutteral *k*,

Who will one day be the elderly man you know,
Word-lover still,
Who, at a late time,
Loves you properly.

IN THE COURTYARD, MUSEUM OF AMERICAN ART

Gravely, the Actor I
Delivers his line in a measured tone,
"You are beautiful."

She is flustered, but only a little.
The Calder sits in the court's corner,
There is tea on the table.

Detached, the Observer I
Is thinking, "He said that well and truly.
He is sincere."

Silence. Was the scene successful?
Apparently, all is well. They go on,
As before, with poetry.

FROM VICKSBURG TO MADRID

This morning, to get me going, you said, "Ready?"
Meaning the Prado. I said, "Just a minute," reading.
You were patient. You couldn't have known
I was back in the role of the boy from Vicksburg,
Sprawled in a chair, absorbed, always a book.
My mother would say, in exasperation,
"He's *always* got his nose stuck in a book."
When she called me for something, I'd whine,
"Just let me finish this chapter." "Robert!" she'd say.
But today it's Madrid, not Vicksburg. You don't resemble
My mother much. Good. Today is better.
Now we'll go and look at the paintings
Done by the great Spaniard, Berenson calls him.
Be uplifted together. And on the way,
Sunshine, crisp fall air, walking with you,
I'll probably dance in the park.

OUR HANDS WERE OCCASIONALLY TOUCHING

Our hands were occasionally touching across the back
      of the couch.
In the warmth and solemnity, you might have said,
"Back then, you told me, I think,
The room lit up when *she* came in."
But I would've said, the answer ready,
Hands touching now,
"Yours is a different light."

THINGS THAT GO ON BETWEEN US

Standing at the elevator, you are saying
I don't have to go with you, down to your car.
But I say, "Who knows what might happen —
Someone may get on the elevator, I might say
Something about this person, walking to your car.
Then you might say something back,
An observation spoken with loving profundity,
Something that shows me again the depths of your heart.
I don't want to miss that."

TWO PARTIES

After those parties, both on the same night,
One small, sober, Apollonian, music
By Mozart strings, the other large,
Frenetic, Dionysian, wild dancing to rock,
We're finally alone together, lie down together,
Under the moving ribs of light on the ceiling.
We touch each other, murmuring gently,
Discussing softly the problems of love and lust,
Our responsibility to each.

AT THE BREAKFAST TABLE

The two of us sitting here, everything good:
The yogurt you mixed with grapes, seedless,
The buttered toast,

The sweet tart jam, the black coffee,
And just to the right on the table, art cards
To be examined,

Mozart is quietly filling the room
With a string quintet, ordered and joyous,
1782,

And above all, you! Your glasses on,
Reading the *Post*, studious now,
The young business woman.

The jam, it seems, is almost used up.
There are one or two jars left in the storeroom,
Then they'll be gone.

THE LAST LETTER

That last letter you wrote me, perhaps
the last you wrote to anyone, ever,
mentioned a college scene: our old friend Hull,
the way he'd sometimes preach when drunk
to friends sitting around in the dormitory —
his oily, caressing voice: "Jesus saves!"
And how he'd always wind up with the tale
of Old Bill Jones, the unrepentant sinner,
"Bill, please come, won't you come?" But Bill
just sat there, of course, and came to his bad end.

Your letters were like that,
almost always a story, something to discuss:
this time the way of Old Bill Jones's going.
No question that Hull used to say, "He stumped his toe,
fell down three flights of stairs, broke his neck . . ."
But then your letter goes on, "and was in hell
in thirty seconds!"
                Sidney, old friend,
Hull never said that. What he said was, believe me,
"and was in hell in thirty minutes!" *Minutes.*
It takes a certain amount of time to be sent to hell:
the sorting of sinners, St. Peter's arraignment,
usually taking hours, but for dour old sinners
shortened to thirty minutes.
Enough of this — for who knew better than you
the importance of small but accurate touches
to a story's perfection — you, tale teller supreme,
master of all raconteurs!

I wanted to tell you this — pupil to master —,
see your smile as you mulled it over,
hear your appraisal, your considered response.
Now we'll never go over it all, chuckling.
We will not sit there, fifty good years between us,
everything straightened out.

III VIEWS

ASPECTS OF A SOUTHERN STORY

I   The story as told

That this black Mississippi woman, untraveled,
standing on the beach at Biloxi, her first sight
of those rounded waters, nothing but water
to the sky's edge —
the small conservative waves curling up
to her shod feet —
and she staring quietly a long time,
and finally saying slowly,
"Ain't near as big as I thought it'd be."

II   The usual telling

The casually dressed white people sitting around
in a southern living room, having their drinks and stories.
Somebody says, "Did I tell you about . . . ?" tells one,
then everyone chuckles, and that one brings on another.
They have this quiet, undiscussed bond: the stories,
usually humorous, some about blacks, not all,
are a way of viewing, and a way of telling each other:
we're all right, we are the story tellers, not told on.
They're fond of the butts of these stories: the ignorant black,
the old maid, the miser, the liar, the hypocrite:
we're here together, they are down there, be thankful.
"Now this black woman, you see, the Dade's nurse,
had her for a long time, they took her to Biloxi . . . "
Not "nigger," these days, usually.

III   The woman

Born in a shack by the Big Black River
into a large family. Name, Alberta Johnson.
After some years of one-room schooling,
was put out to work for the Dades, a rich white family,
as maid, housekeeper, cook, nurse, you name it.
Was honest, dependable. Loved by the Dade children.
Stayed on through the years. Self-respecting,
she was also somewhat outspoken — "speaks her mind,"
the Dades all said, tolerantly. There were, of course,
things not spoken.

IV   The trip

That year she was taken with them to Biloxi, wedged
on the back seat of the car with the younger Dades.
Driving down, there was talk: "Tell us, really, Alberta,
you never have seen the ocean?" "No," she grumped,
"ain't never see'd it. Ain't never wanted to see it."
Secretly, she did.

V   Why alone on the beach?

Mr. Dade, smarter than you might think him,
when he stopped the car, stopped the children from going.
"Let Alberta go. You've seen it plenty of times."

VI   Alberta as stout Cortez

What wild surmise went glimmering,
when she came to that beach, her Darien?

VII Magnitudes

Protagoras taught we size things by ourselves,
saying, reputedly, "Man is the measure of all,"
and therefore Alberta, making her private appraisal
of the restless sea, its magnitude against hers,
doubtless thought it delimited, not so big,
and reported it thus: the size of the sea as she saw it.

VIII Her posture

From the way she stood,
her shoulders back, head high, her face a frown,
surely she showed at least a touch of defiance.
Was Alberta playing folk-hero, defying the deep
by belittling its size?

IX The words she chose

Could have remained unspoken. Or replaced
by words suiting the occasion, with maybe a grin,
like, "Ain't that grand!"
and gratitude for the wondrous privilege granted
by Mr. and Mrs. Dade. Alberta, however,
independent as usual, said something different.

X Alberta as fretted servant

Were her words a way of letting the Dades know,
as she had done in the past, her demand for respect.
But to save face for all, disguised
by a humorous grumpiness?

XI   Alberta the performer

Was Alberta reporter, folk-hero, the fretted servant,
player of multiple roles, and all at once?

XII   The Dade children

Later, alone with their father, said, "Daddy,
don't make fun of Alberta." He smiled and said,
"I won't tell it in front of her."

XIII   Back to the story

From all these ramifications, only the story,
pruned of its non-essentials, simplified
by multiple tellings, survives.

XIV   A loose end

In the story as told, her words were breathed to the air,
with no one to hear. But in fact,
the words were brought forth as they drove away,
when pressed by the children. Mr. Dade, you see,
knew as a southerner he had a *story*,
which, as southerners know,
is subject to rearrangement.

XV   Things missed

THE LOST POEMS

Having for my soul's rescue come to poetry
At a late time, the noon of my life past,
I think of the early poems, the lost ones
Never to be written,
The poems of my 20's and 30's.
Some doubtless naive and stumbling,
Not yet free, but perceptive, a good ear,
Some of them powerful, surely,
Nailing in words some now half-forgotten experience
(The whore with the sullen eyes, naked on the bed,
Says, "Why did you choose me?")
Nothing can be done now, those old poems.
Something I never lived up to.

JANIE

Southern way of talking. "I was flown at by birds,"
She said, explaining her avian antipathy.
Meaning when she was a child. Part of me saw her
Small and cowering under the winged attack.
But that turn of phrase, the effortless use
Of the passive voice, that soft Mississippi tongue —
That was what struck.
Brought me home.

THE HOT WATER JUG (1731)

I am thinking of Chardin looking at a brownish jug
Sitting on a table, beside it a glass
Filled with what seems to be water almost blue.
Lying nearby are a few cloves of garlic,
Cloudy white, and some scattered flower leaves.
He is staring as if somehow these simple objects
Are there for the first time,
Had never been seen before, their exactness,
Their distinction.

MISSISSIPPI JUKEJOINT: HIGHWAY 51

She is talking across the table, over her beer,
And over the jukebox music, "You Are My Sunshine"
(We are getting acquainted),

"Me and my husband, we live down near Pickens,
Right on 51. Whenever we take a notion
To go out juking,

He goes south, toward Canton. Now me,
I come north, this way. That way, you see,
We don't never bother each other."

TODAY'S POETRY : LESSON ONE

The master of all poets could use the line
The multitudinous seas incarnadine.
But we must watch the fustian, must prefer
More Anglo-Saxon usage; mustn't err
By using iambs, pentametric time;
And never ever, if we're serious, rhyme.

MY GRANDSON BILLY

Comes on a visit to me, his first alone,
Dumps his bag at the door, says "Granddad!"
Hugs me properly,
Then, does not
      Take his bag to the bedroom,
      Ask for a coke,
      Go to the bathroom,
      Tell me the family news,
But rather, seeing the books across the room,
Heads straight for the shelves,
Starts looking at titles, scanning
This one, that one . . . .

THE EPISTEMOLOGIST, OVER A BRANDY, OPINING

Relaxing here with brandy and certitude,
Consider our imprecise grasp of things, fuzzy,
Nothing what it seems,

And not even the equations of the scientist — arcane,
Useful in prediction — can convey the confusion, the *buzz*,
Of the hidden complexities,

Simplicity merely being the mind's abstraction
To be able to deal with something. Remember,
Simplicity is parochial.

Think of our isolation! Our blinkered view
Of what's going on around us! It's been set
By millions of years,

So it works well, bringing us food and progeny.
Only sometimes a whiff, something out there,
The message unclear.

> *But perhaps the most important factor . . . was the appeal
> . . . of the pancreatic acinar cell, whose cytoplasm is
> packed with stacked endoplasmic reticulum cisternae
> studded with ribosomes. Its pictures had . . . the effect
> of the song of a mermaid: irresistible and half transparent.*
>
> *George Palade, Biologist*
> *Nobel Lecture, Stockholm, December, 1974*

Good morning. Seats, please.
Today, we have Palade's poem, "The Cell,"
A rather intriguing selection.

The comments you turned in were most disappointing.
Here is a typical one:
"*What* is the pancreatic acinar cell?" My God!
And only last time we discussed Mallarmé
And his words to the Symbolist poets:
"The identity of objects should be revealed gradually.
To *suggest* — that should be the poet's dream."
I will try to say something slowly, carefully.
Please listen.
Rothko is non-objective but significant.
Rimbaud is non-objective but significant.
This poem is non-objective but significant.
Look for the connotations.

It begins:
  But perhaps
A tentative, groping note . . .
  The most important factor
  Was the appeal of the pancreatic acinar cell
Please, remember, connotations.
Pan — Greek, all-embracing.
Creatic — creativity.
Cell — something lowly, a prison.
Can't some of you feel a *suggestion* (Mallarmé's word)
Of deep and pervasive creativity?
And from where? From a low and imprisoned soul.

Continuing:
>*Whose cytoplasm is packed*
>*With stacked endoplasmic reticulum cisternae*
>*Studded with ribosomes.*

We see the cell is full of significance.
Packed, in fact. Stacked and studded.
Note the internal rhyming. The short Anglo-Saxon words
Surrounded by the Latinate. Real toads
For Mr. Palade's imaginary garden.
What? Who? Moore.

And now the conclusion:
>*Its pictures had the effect of the song of a mermaid.*

Palade is not too disdainful of old-fashioned anapests.
>*Irresistible and half transparent.*

A beautiful ending! For the poet, as well as for you,
The object is only dimly discerned.

No questions. All right, one. Eliot?
One can say that Palade's use of the mermaid symbol
(See "Prufrock") is surely not accidental.

Next session, "Sonnet," Tom Clark.
Be prepared to discuss its affinities with "The Cell."
Hint: biological terms. Class dismissed.

CIRCE TO ULYSSES

No,
I'm a good witch, although
What your sailors said
Is true enough, in a way. With my small wand
I changed them into beasts: shape and sound
And all. But not maliciously. Instead,
Before the magic tap, with a long look
I read from each his dark unwritten book
Of lust. His secret hope. And it was granted.
Really, I only gave them what they wanted.

A BIRCH IN WINTER

Suppose I write:
She is a birch in winter, white,
Standing flat
Against the dark amorphous woods.

Suppose somehow, by the way poetry gets printed,
The lines above appear before you, dignified
In black, beautiful print, wide white margins,
Three little lines of trash,

You might surmise, knowing the locale of birches,
This floral vision pierced my own true eyes
Up north, perhaps near Boston, north of Boston,
Stopping by woods on some bright frosty night.
That would be wrong.
It came, easy and soft, between sleeping and waking,
In a warm Virginia bedroom.

You might deduce from the above
I have been one acquainted with the works
Of Mr. Frost. That would be right.

And you could surely make from all of this
That I think there is something more to poetry
Than the metaphorical, pretentious lyric.
That also would be right.

BILLIE HOLIDAY

When I say, stopping the tape,
"The next one coming up, a vintage Billie,
Surpasses all the vocals ever sung,"

And frowning you demur,
Say you should hear it first before commitment,
I grant the surface plausibility

Of what you say: surely
It would apply to questions of judgment, taste.
But what I say is merely a statement of fact.

NOT YET THE DAY

The escalator is taking me slowly down
To the subway platform, everything is in order,
I've done what I came downtown for, my car's at home,
It's not standing somewhere parked on a D.C. street
Till I get back — and it's nice that it's not that day
Going down, yet, when I won't be able to think
Where my car is, whether I even brought it,
Whether I did what I came for — thinking only:
This creaking, moving beast! — why am I here?

MOUNT MCKINLEY

I watch with the rest old snow-white, lordly McKinley,
        Tall in his postcard pride,
Above the obeisant floor of the gray soft clouds,
        In our droning aircraft's ride,
And around me the oh's and ah's of my rapt companions,
        And I think, how can this compare
To one small acid, human, Daumier court-scene,
        Or a simple Van Gogh chair?

CROSSING WOODROW WILSON BRIDGE

The river is white, like Fra Angelico's white,
That is to say, not too white,
Almost an impure white,
Against the dark green shore.

It flows along, relaxed and peaceful, strong
In its impure whiteness.
A comfortable way to be,
Somewhat impure.

OLD KING, STILL KING

I know you are down there, old holdover brain,
Reptilian, mammalian, I can feel your working.
For instance, last night, half asleep,
Trying to make up my mind to go to the bathroom —
Suddenly you gave orders to my body,
It rolled out of bed responding,
I was halfway across the room before I knew it.
On other occasions, you don't need to be told
To set in motion the requisite blood
Into the flaccid tissue.

But tell me, ancient center of things,
Old king, still king,
Your declination over the ages, what of that?
Your power nibbled away
As the neo-cortex expanded, taking over.
Many things, now, consciously planned, not felt.
Reptile to beast to man. Where next?

When that day comes when tumescence is ordered up
By thought, unpricked by emotion,
Then will we still be men?

THE CULPRIT

In a dream my brother dear
Betrays the weakness that I fear.
I do not choose to tell you what
He perpetrates so slyly, but

The fact he wears a sheepish grin
Shows that he hides some truth within
The veil of his duplicity.
Who is Brother, what is he

Who draws me in a small dark door?
Have I seen what's behind before?
What wakes me up before I scream?
Who is unveiled in that dark dream?

THE ARTIST, RESPONDING TO THE WORK OF AN
OLDER CONTEMPORARY

John C. Hodges, known as "Rabbit" to some,
Is sitting alone in a furnished room
In a Boston rooming house. It is 1926.

He is dapper, young, black. Has a thin mustache.
From the case on the floor, he must be a musician.
A phonograph is playing New Orleans jazz,

"Texas Moaner Blues," Clarence William's Blue Five.
It's Bechet that he's listening to, the soprano sax.
Johnnie is tapping his foot,

And from this, and his smile, you might think
He is playing the record because he enjoys the music.
And that's true as far as it goes,

But that's not the point of his listening.
That eruption of gutsiness after the smooth glissando:
How is it done, exactly?

He puts the needle back to the saxophone solo.
That rough vibrato! When the record stops,
He opens the case on the floor, takes out his horn.

SAINT ANTHONY

Those to whom you are important, these days not many,
Think mostly of your temptations, the desert horrors
Of Brueghel, and how you resisted them, triumphed.
"Help me, Saint Anthony!" no doubt some still say.
I do not disparage this, God knows.
We need all the help we can get.

But what I see is you an old man of 90,
Crutch in hand, bearded, vigorous, striding,
Searching for Paul the Hermit. He's old too.
Finally, his cave. Slowly, Paul comes out.
And now a long look in each other's eyes.
You hug each other, your long white beards
Over each other's shoulder. You're both crying.
Now you will live together, two old men,
Fed by a raven. I can hear you saying,
"Paul, what in the world did you do with the pottage?"

PABLO

You were always formidable. Slowly I knew
I had you to contend with, settle with — no soft Renoir
Easy to place, his vapid girlfaces
Candybox. You were

Hard, humorous, talented — my God
How talented! So of course is Dali. But did you see
His flashy Supper? More than talent is required.
Taste. Sensibility.

And at first I was able to dismiss your harsh
Skewed two-eyed profiles. Your publicity aided me against you.
Until on a gallery day, you showed me
What you could do —

A quiet drunk gallery day in Chicago,
Pablo, a quiet day. An acrobat's wife?
Did you have her, Pablo? I wouldn't be surprised.
Your life

Has been full, productive, lived. Work counted.
Always a using up, a move-on, search, frontiers.
I admire you. I admit it. You win. But Pablo,
For your pictures, no tears.

FUNERAL MEDITATION, AS A SONG

Attendance a duty for people who come to this rite,
The eulogy false, condolences only polite,
His mark undistinguished, what he left trifling — still,
Why shouldn't he get the formality most of us will?
               And don't sneer
At the honor we proffer to this man's memory here,
               Nor forget
This ritual tribute is one of the few that we get.
               Even dead,
It's better to have it than rather have nothing instead,
               And indeed,
An occasional mark of respect is what all of us need.
               Yes, indeed,
     In fact, it's what all of us need.

LOOKING FOR OLDNESS

Looking for oldness, sometimes you might see
An old veteran of a house, its upper storey
Over a store. Say Old Town, Alexandria.
And interposing your hand to block the view
Of what's below, for instance cars,
You see things ante-bellum: wagons creaking,
Horses snorting, sparrows foraging
In the street, and in the upstairs window
A girl knitting. Socks, no doubt, and hoping.
To what has she affixed her yearning heart?
That her beau will appear below, strolling along,
Bent on his show. Then she'll pretend not to see him.
And he too her, both of them knowing better.
There he is! Sauntering by, his eyes turned down.
She knits away. What will happen between them?
They both seem certainly there, real,
Alive in that old street.
But when you drop your hand, today takes up
Where it left off. Things fall in place —
Traffic lights, signs, cars —
The window's there, no girl. The house sits.

FRANCE

Landed at Bordeaux once, my first time
To walk on France. Concrete apron, but saw
Grass a short distance away. Walked over, stood there,
Green underfoot. Shoes on, couldn't feel it, of course.
Still, grass, closer to earth. France!

THE OLD LADY

Here's the old lady, dumped by her daughter
In a bookshop tearoom,

Sitting at a table, sipping tea.
Through the window,

The planes dip low toward the airport.
She is watching.

And time passes in the bookshop's somnolence.
Nothing seems happening.

Finally her daughter returns, impatient.
Says, "Ready to go?"

The old lady smiles. "Oh, yes," she answers,
Struggling up,

And throwing her head back, says, with some pride,
"I counted twelve planes."

NOTES

Henry Barry Sargent (1844-1914)
  Holmes is Oliver Wendell Holmes (1841-1935), wounded
  at Ball's Bluff, later the Supreme Court justice.

Touching the Past
  Buddy Bolden, legendary jazz trumpet player in New
  Orleans until about 1907, when he was committed to an
  asylum, was never (it is believed) recorded.

The Brook Cherith
  See I Kings 17:2-7 for Elijah and the brook Cherith.

Lending "The King of the Golden River"
  The tale is by John Ruskin.

From Vicksburg to Madrid
  "The great Spaniard" as Berenson calls him, is of course
  Velasquez.

Two Parties
  For "Apollonian" versus "Dionysian," see Nietzsche's
  The Birth of Tragedy.

Aspects of a Southern Story
  For Alberta as stout Cortez, see Keats's "On First Look-
  Into Chapman's Homer."

The Hot Water Jug (1731)
  The picture is in the Museum of Art, Carnegie Institute,
  Pittsburgh.

Today's Poetry: Lesson One
  Shakespeare's line is from *MacBeth*, Act II, Scene 2.

English 406
  "Real toads," etc. is from Marianne Moore's "Poetry."

Crossing Woodrow Wilson Bridge
  Alberti advised, and Fra Angelico followed the advice,
  that white should never be as bright as possible. See *A
  Pageant of Painting from the National Gallery of Art*,
  ed. Cairns and Walker, p. 22.

The Artist, Responding . . .
    Johnnie Hodges, who acknowledged his debt to Bechet,
    was Duke Ellington's lead alto saxophone for many
    years.

Saint Anthony
    Two pictures, both in the National Gallery, bear on this
    poem: *The Temptation of Saint Anthony*," now attribu-
    ted to "Follower of Breughel," and *The Meeting of St.
    Anthony and St. Paul*, Sassetta and Assistant.

Pablo
    Dali's *The Sacrament of the Last Supper* is in the Na-
    tional Gallery.

ROBERT SARGENT

Robert Sargent, born and educated in the south (New Orleans, Mississippi), came to the Washington area as a Naval officer in World War II and remained as a civil servant until his retirement a few years ago. He began writing poetry in the '50s and has been widely published in literary reviews, including *Prairie Schooner, Antioch Review, California Quarterly, College English, Sou'Wester*, and many others. His first book, *Now Is Always the Miraculous Time*, was published in 1977; his second, *A Woman from Memphis*, in 1979.